# Earth and Sky Cakes

retold by Sheri Reda
illustrated by Bradley H. Clark

MODERN CURRICULUM PRESS
Pearson Learning Group

King Vuong was a splendid king with a kingdom that stretched from the South China Sea in the east to the mountains in the west. The land was rich and lovely and gave its people a good living.

The people of the kingdom harvested bamboo and timber and pulled basket after basket of fish from the sea. They raised rice, beans, and bananas to eat and sell. On Tet, the new year, they feasted to celebrate their happy, peaceful lives.

The king was a great and wise father of four sons. Each son was handsome, smart, and strong. Any one of the princes would make a fine king.

As the king grew older, he realized that he needed to name an heir and wondered whom he should choose. His oldest son was a fine warrior who would keep the kingdom safe from invaders. The people would find that reassuring.

His second son was good at trade and would help the merchants become rich. The people would find that pleasant. His other two sons were very clever and would make life interesting.

The king thought for a long time, then listed the good qualities of all his sons. He knew that each son would make a good ruler, but who would rule most wisely and be best?

Finally, King Vuong decided to hold a contest, so he called his knights together and told them to fetch his sons.

The knights traveled far and wide to reach all the princes. All four sons traveled many days to meet with their father.

The king's oldest son traveled from a castle in the mountains, and the youngest one came from a simple cottage in the country. Yet they all met in the throne room of the palace, each one eager to serve his father.

The king looked down from his throne and smiled with pride at his sons. He knew that all of his sons were fit to be kings, and the sight of them was reassuring to him.

The king lifted his hand to speak. "My beloved sons," the king said, "I wish to create a tradition for Tet, the new year. From this year forward, I want all the people of our kingdom to make a special dish for Tet."

"I hereby challenge you to invent a new food that will be something the people will love to make and eat, and which will become our national food."

The king went on. "Go and think about what our kingdom has to offer, then make a dish from items in the kingdom. Make a food that stands for the greatness of our land. Whoever makes the finest dish will become king after me."

The king nodded his head as a sign that the meeting was over, so his servants opened the door, and the princes prepared to leave. The princes were buzzing with excitement and spoke about fine spices that only grew in faraway valleys. They told about herbs that grew on the cold, forbidding mountaintops.

The king's oldest son called for maps and a travel party so that he could travel to the farthest borders in search of fine, unusual foods. The king's second son visited every market and every harbor to collect the finest herbs, spices, and foods he could find for sale. The king's third son called upon the kingdom's best chefs. "Teach me all you know," he said, "as I must become the best cook in the kingdom!"

The fourth son also prepared to leave the palace. First, he paid his respects to the people there, then he stopped to visit the nurse who had fed him, and he spoke with some of the tutors who had taught him to read, write, and study. He visited the man in the stable who took care of his horse and taught him to ride, and he shook the gnarled hands of the workers who had sewn his clothes. Finally, the prince made his way home to his cottage, having no idea what dish he would make.

The youngest prince sighed with disappointment as he would have liked to serve as king. Mostly, he would have liked to please his father, but he didn't think he could win.

He didn't know any faraway valleys or high mountains, nor did he know any important people. He lived a simple country life, as his wisest teacher had taught him to do before she died.

The prince then thought of this wise teacher. She had taken him to the cottage in the country to teach him how to live simply and had told him, many times, that glory and riches are not important. She had taught him to love the land and the people who worked it. She had even taught him how to farm, cook, and sew. When she died, the prince had stayed at the cottage, at first because it reminded him of his teacher, but later on, because he grew to love the simple life.

The prince loved where he lived because of its forests and the swaying banana trees. He loved the huge banana leaves, which people used for plates, and the square little patches of farmland, the bean fields, and the rice paddies.

The prince loved the land, but he wondered what it had to offer. It did not have the spices of the faraway valley, or the tender herbs of the mountaintops, or fancy dishes made by famous chefs.

The youngest prince did not give up, though. Day after day, he thought about the contest as he worked his land, made his meals, tended the cottage, and sewed his clothes. In the afternoons, he wandered in the forest, searching for new foods. He walked the well-tended fields, thinking about what to do, but still, no answers came to him.

Harvest began and ended, and still, the youngest prince had no answers. Tet approached, and the prince began to despair, wondering whether he would have to return to the palace empty-handed.

One evening, the prince brought the last of the beans and rice into storage and then stood before the harvest. He thought that the land and the sky and the growing things were the jewels of the land, but he realized that the people at court could not see their beauty.

That night, the prince had a wonderful dream. His wisest teacher appeared to him. She was very young, but her hands were gnarled from hard work.

"Oh," she said, "I have worked so hard to grow rice and beans, which will feed and nourish the people I protect and serve. They are finer and more important than all the warriors, traders, and clever men in the world."

When the prince awoke, he knew what he
wanted to do, so he gathered some fresh banana
leaves from a tree near his cottage. Then he cooked
some tender, fresh rice from his field and mixed it
with cooked beans.

The prince wrapped the rice and beans in the banana leaves, making different shapes with different leaves. Some were round, like the sky overhead, and some were square, like the fields. The prince baked the cakes in his brick oven, then he took them out and unwrapped them. The banana leaves had dyed the cakes a lovely green, like the trees. The prince tasted one. Its fresh, delicate flavor delighted him, so he decided to bring the cakes to the palace. He decorated a plate with banana leaves and began to make more of the cakes.

On the day of Tet, the palace was filled with amazing dishes. Amazing sights and smells filled the air of the great hall.

The hall was filled with chatter, too, as the princes told about their foods. Some dishes were spicy, and others were mild. The oldest prince made a dish with rare spices, the second prince made a dish with tender herbs, and the third prince made a dish that looked beautiful. All the princes were bursting with pride. The youngest prince looked down at his plate of simple rice cakes and blushed. He wanted to run back home, but it was too late.

After everyone found a place in the great hall, the king came in. He tasted each dish. He praised his oldest son for finding herbs and spices that grew on the borders of the kingdom, and he praised his second son for buying only the finest ingredients. He praised his third son for making a dish that was a delight to the eye as well as the mouth.

The king finally came to the youngest son, who held out his plate of simple cakes. "I call the square ones earth cakes," he said, "and the round ones are called sky cakes. I made them from the rice and beans in my fields."

The king looked down at the simple cakes, then he looked at his youngest son. The king's expression suddenly changed. The prince blushed, as he thought his father was laughing at him. Still, the king tasted a cake and praised the firmness and freshness of the beans and rice.

The next day, the king called his sons into the throne room and announced to them, "I have found our next king." Then he called his sons to stand before the throne.

"All of my sons have found wonders in my kingdom," he said, "but only one of you honored the simple things that make the kingdom great. Only one of you invented a dish everyone in the kingdom can make. My youngest son has done this and therefore has the wisdom to be king."

The other princes bowed to the youngest prince. They would each receive from him important jobs in the new kingdom.

The new king advised his brothers well and ruled his people with love. Every year at Tet, he invited everyone in the kingdom to help him make earth and sky cakes to celebrate the new year. Those are the very same earth and sky cakes the people of Vietnam make today, in praise of King Vuong, and every ancestor who came before them.